I Wonder Why

Dinosaurs

flip the flaps

Judy Allen and Tudor Humphries

KINGFISHER

Contents

KINGFISHER

First published 2008 by Kingfisher
an imprint of Macmillan Children's Books
a division of Macmillan Publishers Limited
20 New Wharf Road, London N1 9RR
Basingstoke and Oxford
www.panmacmillan.com

Associated companies throughout the world

Consultant: Michael J Benton, Department of Earth Sciences, University of Bristol

ISBN 978-0-7534-1616-7

Copyright © Macmillan Children's Books 2008

9 8 7 6 5 4 3 2 1
1TR/1207/LFG/UNTD/140MA/C

A CIP record is available from the British Library.

Printed in China

How to say dinosaur names

Allosaurus 'al-oh-sore-us'
Ankylosaurus 'an-kie-loh-sore-us'
Archaeopteryx 'ark-ee-opt-er-ix'
Avimimus 'ah-vee-meem-us'
Brachiosaurus 'brak-ee-oh-sore-us'
Ceratosaurus 'keh-rat-oh-sore-us'
Compsognathus 'komp-sog-nath-us'
Diplodocus 'di-plod-oh-kuss'
Dromaeosaur 'drom-ee-oh-sore-us'
Edmontosaurus 'ed-mon-toe-sore-us'
Gallimimus 'gal-lee-meem-us'
Iguanodon 'ig-wha-noh-don'
Maiasaura 'my-ah-sore-rah'
Mamenchisaurus 'mah-men-chi-sore-us'
Parasaurolophus 'pa-ra-saw-rol-off-us'
Polacanthus 'pol-ah-kan-thus'
Protoceratops 'pro-toe-serra-tops'
Psittacosaurus 'sit-ak-oh-sore-us'
Stegoceras 'ste-gos-er-as'
Stegosaurus 'steg-oh-sore-us'
Struthiomimus 'struth-ee-oh-meem-us'
Triceratops 'try-serra-tops'
Tyrannosaurus rex 'tie-ran-oh-sore-us rex'
Velociraptor 'vel-oss-ee-rap-tor'

3

When did the dinosaurs live?

Dinosaurs lived long ago – further back in time than any of us can imagine. They were here before there were any horses or dogs or cats. They were here before there were any people.

Tyrannosaurus rex

4

1. The word 'dinosaur' means 'terrible lizard'.

2. No. Lizards are different from dinosaurs. A lizard's legs spread out sideways, but a dinosaur's legs go straight down.

3. Yes. Some walked on two legs and some on four. There were small ones, big ones, spiky ones, smooth ones, scaly ones and some with hair or feathers.

Some types of dinosaur

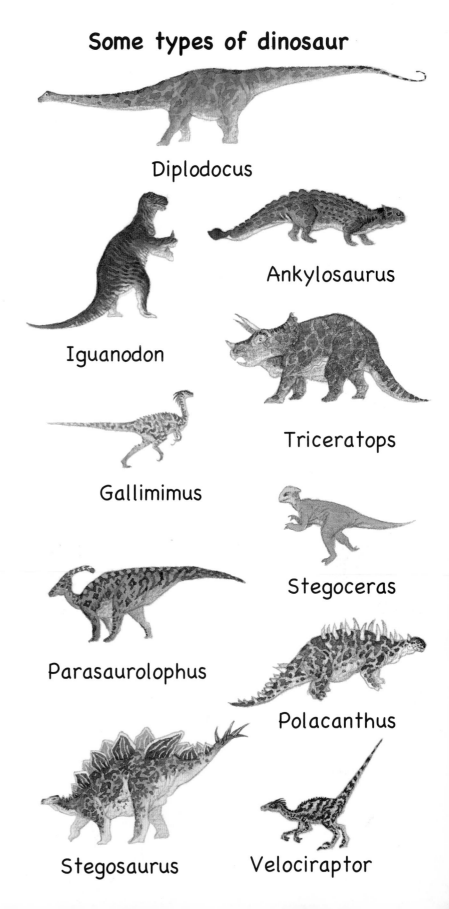

Diplodocus

Ankylosaurus

Iguanodon

Triceratops

Gallimimus

Stegoceras

Parasaurolophus

Polacanthus

Stegosaurus

Velociraptor

Food

Dinosaurs ate plants or meat, or both – just like animals do today. The plant-eaters ate roots, the leaves of plants and trees, and fruit. The meat-eaters ate the plant-eaters and each other.

Protoceratops, a plant-eater, eating leaves

1. No. Dinosaurs that ate from the tree-tops had very long necks.

2. No. Grass did not exist when the dinosaurs were alive.

3. Meat-eaters hunted other dinosaurs. Some hunted alone, and others hunted in packs. They were very fierce.

Mamenchisaurus eating from a tree-top

Fighting back

Plant-eating dinosaurs were hunted by meat-eaters so some had body armour. They had horns or spikes or tails like whips to help fight off attacks. Some lived in big groups to protect each other.

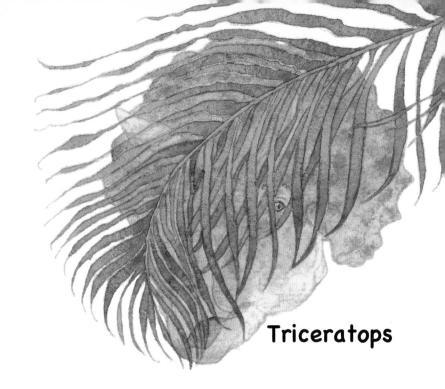

Triceratops

Diplodocus under attack

Ceratosaurus

8

Stegosaurus senses danger...

1. Triceratops had hard and bony frills around its neck. It also had three horns on its head.

2. Stegosaurus had four spikes on the end of its tail and some spikes on its back. It could lash out with its spiky tail.

turns its back...

3. Diplodocus could use its long tail to whip attackers and knock them down.

Ceratosaurus
knocked down by tail

and swings its tail!

9

Big and small

Dinosaurs came in many different sizes. Some were enormous – much, much bigger than elephants. Some were small – no bigger than chickens – and there were all sizes in between.

Brachiosaurus skeleton in a museum

1. The biggest plant-eating dinosaur we know about is Brachiosaurus. It was 23 metres long and 12 metres high.

2. The meat-eaters had big teeth. The plant-eaters had small teeth and the duck-billed dinosaurs had no teeth at all.

3. The smallest dinosaur we know about is Compsognathus, which was about the size of a crow.

Compsognathus skeleton

Dinosaur teeth

Allosaurus was a meat-eater

big teeth

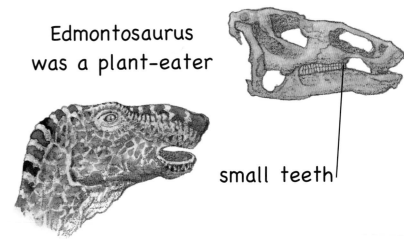

Edmontosaurus was a plant-eater

small teeth

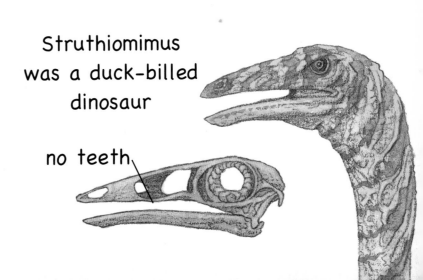

Struthiomimus was a duck-billed dinosaur

no teeth

Babies

Dinosaurs scraped nests in earth or sand, and laid eggs in them. Some covered the eggs to hide them and keep them warm. Some sat on their eggs, just as chickens and other birds do today.

Protoceratops on top of its nest

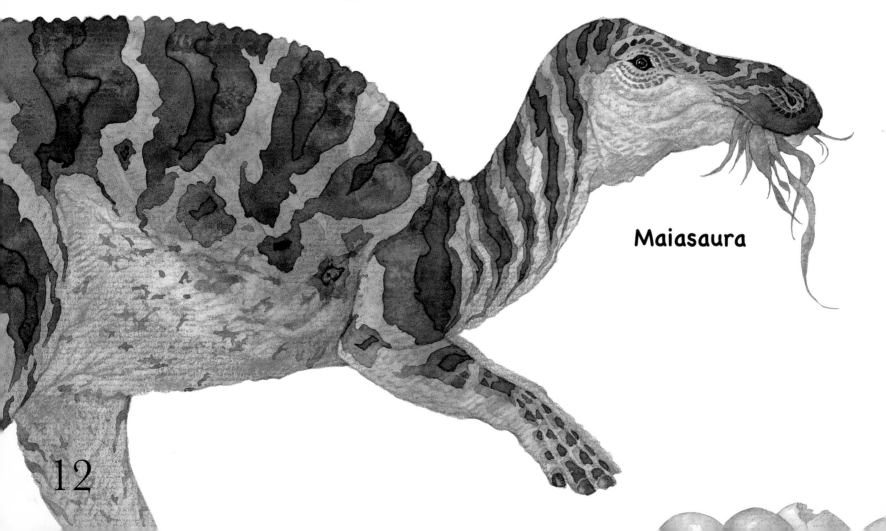

Maiasaura

12

1. Only small dinosaurs sat on their eggs. They were not heavy enough to break them.

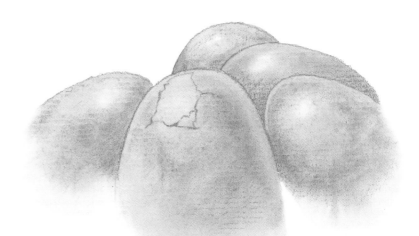

Psittacosaurus egg cracks and...

2. No. When they were ready, the babies broke out of the eggs themselves.

a head pops out!

3. Some dinosaurs, like the Maiasaura, fed their young. But some dinosaur babies had to find their own food.

The baby then breaks out of the egg.

What happened to the dinosaurs?

A huge asteroid crashed into the earth. There was a great explosion. Dust filled the air so it was as dark as night. Huge waves and earthquakes rocked the land. It was the end of the terrible lizards.

Edmontosaurus grazing

Dromaeosaur

14

1. An asteroid is a piece of rock that travels through space.

2. No, only some. Most of the dinosaurs were killed by earthquakes, drowned by huge waves and choked by dust.

3. Yes. Some dinosaurs changed – over a very long time – into all the birds we see today.

Changing from dinosaur to bird

Avimimus was a dinosaur that looked a bit like a bird.

Archaeopteryx was the first bird. It lived with the dinosaurs.

Here are some of the birds that live today. 15

How do we know about dinosaurs?

Sometimes, when a dinosaur died, mud covered its body and, over millions of years, it turned into a stone fossil. 'Fossil' means 'dug up' and a lot of fossil dinosaurs have been discovered.

Parasauralophus body lying in wet mud

palaeontologists digging for fossils

16

1. A fossil dinosaur looks like a skeleton. Sometimes only part of it is ever found.

2. Scientists who know a lot about fossils dig up dinosaurs. These scientists are called palaeontologists ('pa-lee-on-toll-oh-jists').

3. Fossilized footprints have been found that show where dinosaurs walked.

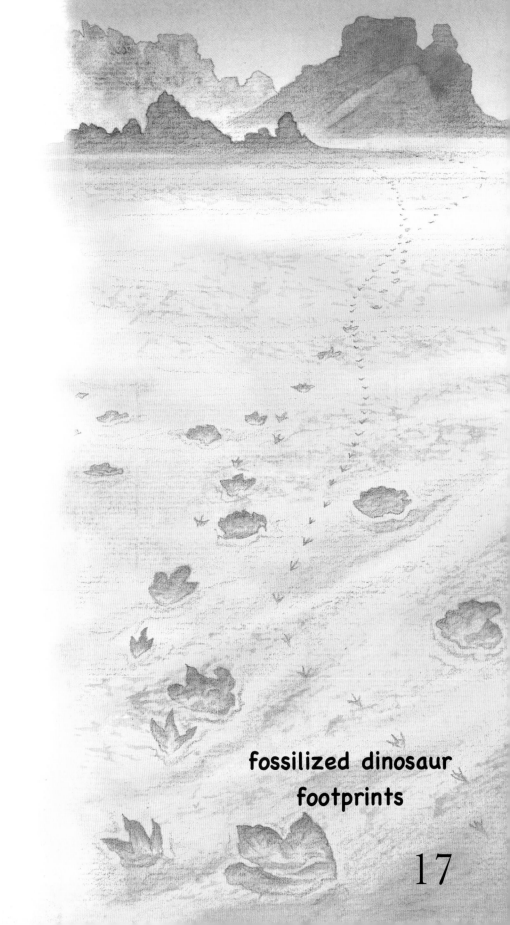

fossilized dinosaur footprints

Index